Thank God For That!

Pr 

ian faith

Tim Mayfield

with James Jones and 'Taffy' Davies

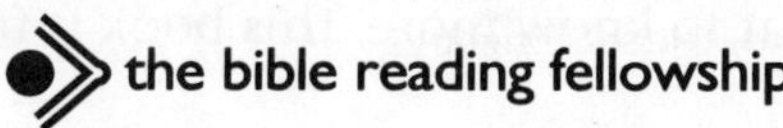

1 Thank God for that

It's the last minute of the Cup Final. Your team is grimly defending a 1–0 lead. Oh no! The ball is hurtling towards the net! The keeper leaps across to it, every muscle straining, just gets his fingertips to it and it passes harmlessly by the post. *'Thank God for that!'*

You're walking down the High Street, when suddenly you realize you've left your handbag in McDonald's, complete with purse, car keys, and cashcard. You sprint back down the street, your heart pounding, and press your face against the glass. Phew! It's still there. *'Thank God for that!'*

We say those words without thinking sometimes. So let's think about them for a moment. If we do, we realize that we can say them in a completely different way . . .

- We've just had a baby . . . *Thank God for that.*
- The operation was a great success . . . *Thank God for that.*
- Look at that fantastic sunset . . .*Thank God for that.*
- I feel glad to be alive . . . *Thank God for that.*

The list could go on for ever. There is so much to thank God for. God is not mean and tight-fisted. The Bible's pictures of him suggest . . .

- The GOOD FATHER, who protects, provides for and forgives his children.
- The HOST, who loves to throw wide the doors and have a party.
- The FARMER, who scatters seed around in a crazy, generous way.

Maybe you've felt that generous love, and have been drawn to church to thank God. Perhaps you were married there, and you want to thank God for sex, and laughter and a new home. Perhaps you've just become parents and are bowled over by the miracle of your first child, so you've come for a christening. Or perhaps you've been drawn here by the story of friends who have discovered that God is good.

Whatever the reason: if you've begun to see the work of God around you and want to know more, this book is for you. *Welcome!*

- List in order of priority the things that mean most to you, that you want to thank God for . . .

Children	*Music*	....	....
Your partner	*The countryside*	....	....
Your friends	*Your job*	....	....
Sport	*Other ...*	....	....

READ:

Shout for joy to the Lord, all the earth . . . Enter his gates with thanksgiving and his courts with praise; give thanks to him and praise his name. For the Lord is good and his love endures for ever.
(Psalm 100:1, 4–5)

PRAY:

Lord God,
There is so much to thank you for.
Help me to live a life of thankfulness,
and not to take anything for granted. Amen.

2 How did I get here?

It was dawn, and the great wide beach was deserted. On the fresh wind, huge pillars of cloud moved steadily inland. Waves crashed on the shore. At the water's edge a flock of sandpipers flashed low over the sea. And in his sling, round my neck, my six-week-old son was fast asleep. I stopped to look down at him. My mind went back to the joy of his birth and I had a great rush of faith: I knew that I was looking at the work of a creator.

Not everyone agrees, of course. It's very popular today to believe that we 'just happened'. But it takes a lot of believing. You have to believe that . . .

- Everything that exists just popped up from nowhere.
- Then, over a period, it got so developed that it began to walk around, understand a difference between right and wrong, and feel things like 'love' and 'courage'.

It's a tall order! Christians think so. Week by week they say that they 'believe in God . . . maker of heaven and earth, of all that is . . .'

And there are good reasons for saying that. Boil a kettle. The kettle gets hot because of electricity from steam-driven turbines. The steam comes from water heated by coal, the coal comes from trees and the trees come from seeds. But where did the seeds come from? And who put life in the seed? Who started the whole business?

How did I get here? The Christian confidently answers, 'I was made by someone'. And that 'someone' the Bible calls 'God'.

READ:

Ever since God created the world, his everlasting power and deity have been there for the mind to see in the things he has made.
(Romans 1:20)

PRAY:

Father,
thank you for the beauty of the world and for the gift of life.
Teach me to see your hand in all that you have made. Amen.

On the 0–10 scales, put a cross that shows how much these things make you think there is a God . . .

Things have a design, there must be a designer.

0 1 2 3 4 5 6 7 8 9 10

There must be more to life than what we see.

0 1 2 3 4 5 6 7 8 9 10

The world must have a beginning and an end.

0 1 2 3 4 5 6 7 8 9 10

I just have a gut feeling, deep inside.

0 1 2 3 4 5 6 7 8 9 10

Nature is too beautiful to be here by chance.

0 1 2 3 4 5 6 7 8 9 10

3 *Why did I get here?*

Alison struggled onto the bus with her shopping, found an empty seat and sat down. She ached all over, and was filled with a deep sadness. On the seat in front a young Mum was cradling her baby. They were gazing at each other, and, as Alison watched, the baby's face lit up in a series of brilliant smiles. She looked out of the window and her mind began to wander. She'd been married to John for nine years. Why could they not have children? She longed to know a mother's love for her child . . . tried to guess what it might be like.

That moment on the bus seemed worlds away as John and Alison ran up the stairs into the bathroom. 'If it's blue, I'm pregnant!' she said. (They'd done the test so often now.) She grabbed the plastic stick (three! two! one! zero!) and ripped it out of the pot. They could hardly believe their eyes. The tip was a deep, rich, unmistakable blue. Their long, long wait was nearly over.

The months passed. Little Natalie was born. They held her in their arms. Before, they'd only been able to guess about this love. Now, it was real.

John and Alison and Natalie are windows into God. The Bible tells us that 'God is love'. And love longs to have someone to love. So God made a race of people designed to enjoy his love. That's why we're here. To be loved by God and to love him in return.

READ:

[Someone once asked Jesus] 'Which is the most important law of all?' [He thought for a moment and then replied] '. . . Love the Lord your God with all your heart and with all your soul and with all your mind and with all your strength. The second is this: love your neighbour as yourself.' (Mark 12:28–31)

When two people are in love they want to

...... *Be together.*

...... *Do things together.*

...... *Forgive each other.*

...... *Start a family.*

...... *Make things together.*

...... *Share what they've got.*

...... *Make love.*

...... *Protect each other.*

...... *Respect each other.*

...... *Dance for joy!*

List these in order of priority.

God gave us this ability to love. God is full of love. He loved to make us. He made us for love.

PRAY:

Lord, is it true?
That the reason we're here is to be loved and to love?
If so, I've wasted so much time chasing the wrong thing.
I'm sorry, Lord. Teach me to love.
In Jesus' name. Amen.

4 *Free to choose*

If God made us to love him . . . what went wrong? Something pretty awful happened somewhere along the line, because the world as we know it has more than its fair share of hatred and pain. Why? Why all this in a world made of love?

Well, you cannot force anyone to love you. Try it sometime. Try forcing someone who doesn't love you to love you after all. Or try making a robot love you. In both cases the end result isn't 'love', because real love has to be freely given.

So God gave us the greatest and most dangerous gift of all: the freedom to choose. Having created the world God 'stood back', because love can't force anybody to love.

It's a dangerous gift though. Real freedom brings with it the real chance that it will be used wrongly. If we're free to love him, we're free not to love him, and the history of the world is tragically full of people who've chosen that second freedom. We're free to choose. Free to love him. Free not to love him. Free to decide for him. Free to decide against him. Free even to shirk that decision. But God calls each of us to use our freedom responsibly. It's up to us.

READ:

This day I call heaven and earth as witnesses against you that I have set before you life and death, blessings and curses. Now choose life! So that you and your descendants may live, and that you may love the Lord your God, listen to his voice, and hold fast to him. For the Lord is your life. . . . (Deuteronomy 30:19–20)

☐ A father loved his children so much he was frightened they might harm themselves one day. He was especially afraid that they might leave home and get into bad company. So after school every day he locked them up at home and refused ever to let them out.

Using all the letters below once, and the key letter three times find two words that describe such a person . . .

T	S	E	O	N	A
	M	R	Y	N	R

1. _ (7)

2. _ (6)

Love means giving people freedom.

PRAY:

Thank you that I'm free, Lord.
Free to love you or to turn my back on you.
I'm tired of that second freedom, Lord:
help me to choose the first.
Set my heart on fire with love for you.

5 *Home or Away?*

Jesus often stressed this choice that we all have. One of his most famous stories about choice is the one we call 'The Prodigal Son'.

A man had two sons. One of them decided he'd had enough of his father, demanded his inheritance and cleared off, as far away from him as he could. (In fact, he wished his dad were dead, and wanted the contents of his will there and then.)

The Prodigal Son had a choice: to stay . . . or to go. He went. The relationship between the father and his son was broken: 'The younger son got together all he had, and set off for a distant country' (Luke 15:13).

We call the stories Jesus told 'parables'. And a parable is a story with a cutting edge, a story with more to it than meets the eye. It tells us something about ourselves. Like the Prodigal Son, we use our freedom every day to get our own way. We walk out on God. He made us to enjoy his company; we've all decided not to. The human family is quite simply 'away from home'.

That's what Christians mean when they say the word 'sin'. Sin is not just something that we do. It's what we *are:* runaways — people who've turned our backs on God. And we're all 'sinners'.

READ:

There is no difference, for all have sinned and fall short of the glory of God. (Romans 3:22–23)

In the lines that follow put a tick or a cross if this applies to you. Don't go on to the next until you've done the one before . . .

.... 1. *Ignoring my conscience.*

.... 2. *Forgetting to thank God.*

.... 3. *Keeping everything to myself.*

.... 4. *Forgetting the people who starve.*

.... 5. *Worshipping something other than God.*

.... 6. *Hurting others when I don't get my way.*

.... 7. *Being reluctant to forgive.*

PRAY:

Lord, I've run away from you.
At so many times and in so many ways I've run away.
Now I'm beginning to hear you call me back.
Go on calling, Lord. Amen.

In the Distant Country

It was a sunny September afternoon, and I sat back to watch the box. I'd had my heart set on this programme for days . . . and nothing was going to get in the way. I'd even pulled all the curtains, because the sun was shining on the screen.

Then the doorbell rang. It was some friends: Mum, Dad and three children. 'Hello!' they smiled. 'We've just come to see you.' There was a pause. I panicked. 'Ummm . . . Sorry! We're just going out!' Heartbroken, I went back into the living room. The dark, closed-in space was a symbol of narrow, tight-fisted meanness. And I was ashamed.

Shame and guilt are very common human experiences. One of the Sunday supplements devoted twenty pages to the subject and concluded that 'only saints and psychopaths fail to experience guilt: for the rest of us, it's an inescapable part of the human condition'.

So why are we so guilty? What is it about us that makes us so ashamed sometimes? Why was I so ashamed that sunny afternoon? Because I'd put 'me' first and lied to my friends?

Yes. Self-centredness is a good way of describing 'sin'. We are designed to put God at the centre, but we've wandered away from him, so something else is now at the centre. Ourselves. But because 'ourselves' are so flawed, we end up feeling guilty.

Sin and guilt spoil who we are. They rob us of the peace God has for us. Once again we are the Prodigal Son. At home he had had all he needed. Alone in the distant country, his money gone, 'he went and hired himself out . . . to feed pigs. He longed to fill his stomach with the pods that the pigs were eating, but no one gave him anything' (Luke 15:15–16).

We've all hurt people at some time or other. In the box below, write the initials of those people.

Now pray:

Lord, have mercy.
Christ, have mercy.
Lord, have mercy.

7 *The great divorce*

Here are fourteen different groups of people. Put them into seven pairs of opposites . . .

Whites, capitalists, Russians, Catholics, Socialists, bosses, Communists, blacks, Americans, West, Protestants, East, Trade Unionists, Conservatives.

e.g. West — East

______________ ______________

______________ ______________

______________ ______________

______________ ______________

______________ ______________

______________ ______________

Sometimes the groups of people in the pairs hate each other, because sin divides people. We've already seen how sin is a broken relationship with God, and that it spoils who we are. It also cuts us off from each other . . .

I had to blink in amazement, rub my eyes, and look again before I believed it. But then I did. Pinned to the front door of a house in Bristol was a notice. It said: 'Danger. Stay Away. Dog That Bites. This Means YOU. Nobody welcome. Keep Out.'

I was tempted to laugh at first. But really we have to laugh on the other side of our faces, because that notice, although extreme, tells us something about the way we all are. We find it hard to get on with each other. We put up lots of barriers, but we get angry even with the people we love most. There were 154,000 divorces in the UK in 1987. Violence in the home is on the increase. And every year around the world thousands die in wars.

We can't get on with each other. That's why in church we not only confess that we've sinned against God, but also against each other 'in thought, word and deed'.

READ:

[Jesus said] 'From within, from men's hearts, come evil thoughts, lust, theft, murder, adultery, greed, injustice, lying, indecency, envy, slander, arrogance and folly. All these evil things come from within, and they are what defile a person.' (Mark 7:21–23)

A bleak picture? Maybe. But if the cap fits, let's wear it . . . and do something about it.

Here is the list that Jesus mentioned. Write next to them their opposites . . .

Evil thoughts ....

Theft	*Lust* ....
Adultery	*Murder* ....
Injustice	*Greed* ....
Indecency	*Lying* ....
Slander	*Envy* ....
Folly	*Arrogance* ....

PRAY:

Father God,
I hold out to you your broken world.
Forgive me for my part in breaking it,
and please begin to mend it . . . through me. Amen.

What is God like?

The sound of infant wailing drifted in from the garden. Tony jumped up and ran to the door. Despite many warnings, Mark, his four-year-old son had been climbing up the tree. A slip. A fall. And now Mark lay in a crumpled heap on the ground. Tony ran down the path, gathered him into his arms, and carried him inside.

Ten minutes later, his wounds safely bathed and cradling a warm mug of Ribena, Mark sat on his Dad's knee. He loved the feel of the strong arms gently rocking him and his eyes filled again with tears: 'Sorry, Daddy'. Tony hugged his son to him, kissed his head, and thought he'd never loved him more, than at that moment.

A good father loves to protect his children, to provide for them, to forgive them. And as it sets about showing us what God is like, the Bible often starts with that picture: 'God is like . . . a very good human father. Only he is more than that. He is the perfect father.' Every picture of God as father in the Bible joyfully shouts out the good book's central message: GOD LOVES YOU. He loves you more than anyone has ever loved you. And his arms of love are waiting to hold you.

Jesus knew that. It was his central message too. He often got that message across with the eye of the cartoonist . . .

READ:

'Which of you, if his son asks for bread, will give him a stone? Or if he asks for fish, will give him a snake? If you, then, though you are bad, know how to give good gifts to your children, how much more will your Father in heaven give good gifts to those who ask him!' (Matthew 7:9–11)

The key words there are 'how much more'. I love my wife. I love my children. But I know that my love is only a pale shadow of the love that burns away in the heart of God. GOD LOVES US. And when we really grasp that, and really believe it, nothing can ever be the same again.

☐ **Write the word 'God' into the blanks in St Paul's famous description of love to find out what God is like . . .**

.... is patient, ... is kind; .... does not envy

.... does not boast, ... is not proud. .... is not rude,

.... is not self-seeking, ... is not easily angered,

.... keeps no record of wrongs. .... does not delight in evil

but rejoices in the truth. .... always protects, always trusts,

always hopes, always perseveres. .... never lets us down.'

PRAY:

Almighty God, you have made us for yourself,
and our hearts are restless till they find their rest in you.
Give us, we pray, such an understanding of your love
that our lives may be full of your peace. Amen.

9 *The brilliant fire*

They didn't know it, of course, but Mum was watching them. Watching as two of her sons ganged up on a third. Teasing led to name-calling. Name-calling to bullying. And now hot tears of rage and shame were streaming down Graham's face. Mum had seen enough. She slammed the back door, marched down the garden, took an ear apiece of the guilty parties, and dragged them inside to bed.

Many people today have a wishy-washy view of love. But to be truly loving in this instance, Mum had to take action. She had to step in. She had to stop the fighting, protect the innocent party and punish the guilty. And many people today want God to be like that. They point to pictures of starving Ethiopian children and ask, 'Why doesn't God do something about it?' They want God to be like the Mum in our story.

The thing is . . . he is! God's love is not to be confused with wishy-washy romance. It burns with a brilliant fire. And at the heart of God's love is his justice, the action he takes against everything that spoils his creation.

READ:

Let the heavens rejoice, let the earth be glad; let the sea resound, and all that is in it; let the fields be jubilant, and everything in them. Then all the trees of the forest will sing for joy. They will sing before the Lord, for he comes. He comes to judge the earth. (Psalm 96:11–13)

No more terrorism! No more rape! No more child abuse! No wonder the earth rejoices. But before we look forward too keenly to God's judgement, let's think again. For which of us is able to face the brilliant fire of God's justice with complete confidence? Who is completely sure that he has done nothing wrong? That he has done everything in his power to work with God for a better world? Thank God that as his love flames out in justice, at the same time it pours itself out in mercy. The life and death of Jesus is the story of how that happened. Read on.

❑ **Imagine you are God. Out of love you made the world. In the box below write a list of things in that world that anger you.**

PRAY:

Thank you, Lord, for the brilliant fire of your justice.
Let the flame burn brighter today,
that the nations may show your love for the poor. Amen.

10 Just like his Dad

Every December, people do a very strange thing. Everyone rushes out and buys a fir tree and stands it in the corner of the living room. They develop a sudden craving for turkey, not having touched the stuff all year. And they lead their children to believe that a jolly red man will come down the chimney laden with presents. WHY?

Good question. Christmas today is in danger of becoming a celebration without a centre. We know we're supposed to be happy, but we've forgotten why, and Christmas is a busy time for the Marriage Guidance people and for the Samaritans.

So what are we celebrating? We're celebrating that God came to earth: that Jesus of Nazareth was no ordinary human being but that he was 'just like his Dad', so that if we want to know what God is like, we look at Jesus.

READ:

[Paul writes] He is the image of the invisible God . . . in him all the fullness of God lives in bodily form. (Colossians 1:15, 2 :9)

Sunday by Sunday we agree with Paul. We say that 'we believe in . . . Jesus . . . true God from true God . . . of one being with the Father'. And that's worth celebrating! God came to earth on a great

mission of love and forgiveness. From the beginning he'd poured himself out in love for us. Now he did that perfectly: a baby lying in the arms of a Palestinian girl in some forgotten corner of the Roman Empire. Jesus in the straw was God, having given up everything to side with the poor, the homeless, the defenceless and the weak. He is love. Happy Christmas!

❑ **Find a coin, and place it under this page in the square.**

Now with a pencil, rub over it. The image of the invisible coin comes through onto the page. Whoever looks at the page can see the coin.

St Paul, writing to the Colossians, has a very special description of Jesus. He says he is 'the image of the invisible God' (1:15). The image of the invisible God has come to us in the person of Jesus. Whoever looks at Jesus can see God, because he is 'just like his Dad'.

PRAY:

Lord Jesus,
you lay in a wooden manger.
You died on a wooden cross.
I kneel with the kings and the shepherds
and add my 'thank you' to theirs. Amen.

11 *Helping the hopeless*

Who's the 'best' person you've ever met? Write his or her name in this space .... Now write down three things that make that person 'different'.

....

....

....

Simon was 'different'. He was my boss for seven months at a Night Shelter for homeless people. And during that time, to remind him of the suffering of the poor, he never wore socks or shoes. (On the tramps' grapevine they called him 'Simon Barefoot'.) Every Monday he fasted — the money went to 'War on Want'. He only had two sets of clothes. And by his words and his example he drew the very best out of his workmates, roughly challenging them to live up to what they believed. I can never quite forget Simon. He was one of the best and most disturbing influences of my life.

Jesus was 'different' too. With him, too, people had that feeling of being with someone special, someone out of the ordinary. So crowds flocked after him, eager to catch a glimpse of this 'different' man, and to hear him speak. When they got there, they saw him care for people who had no hope. They saw him . . .

- Heal the blind, the deaf, the paralysed.
- Touch 'untouchable' lepers.
- Have meals with 'rejected' people.
- Drive out evil spirits from the possessed.

No wonder the crowds flocked to him. Here was someone different, someone special. Someone who spent himself in helping the hopeless.

READ:

A leper came to him. Kneeling down he begged him: 'If you want to, you can make me clean'. And filled with hurting love, Jesus reached out his hand, touched the man, and said, 'I do want to. Be clean!' Immediately the leprosy left him, and he was healed.
(Mark 1:40–42)

PRAY:

Lord,
you were simply too
'different' weren't you?
And in the end we
crucified you.
But the world needs
'different' people, Jesus.
I'm ready. Use me. Amen.

12 *Why, Why, Why?*

Part of the work I do is to take funerals. I always meet the grieving relatives before the service. The question that's often on their lips is 'why?' . . .

• Why, if God loves me, did my baby die?

• We were looking forward so much to Harry retiring: his heart attack came two weeks before he did. Why?

• If God is a God of love, why is there cancer in the world?

Why? Why? Why? And if we're honest, we have to say simply, 'I don't know. I don't know why your little baby died.' And it's a very heartless (or glib) person who would say they did. The question of suffering is one to which we have no answers . . . yet.

But that doesn't mean we hang our heads in despair, feeling God has abandoned us. There is a clue, which helps us wait for a fuller answer. The clue is the death of Jesus on the cross.

READ:

From the sixth hour until the ninth hour darkness came over all the land. About the ninth hour Jesus cried out in a loud voice, 'My God, my God, why have you forsaken me?' . . . And when Jesus had cried out again in a loud voice, he gave up his spirit.
(Matthew 27:45–46, 50)

Crucifixion was one of the most awful ways of dying. Large iron spikes were driven through the victim's wrists and ankles. They pinned him to large cross-pieces of wood. And there the victim hung until he finally died. But remember who was on that cross: the Son of God. And as he hung there, Jesus took suffering into the very heart of God. No one needs to tell God about suffering. No one who's hurting need think he's far away. He knows all about it, because he's been there. And he's with you—hurting with you—now.

In these three boxes, make a note of three sad and painful times.

Now take time to read them out slowly to God. After each one, pause and ask God, *'Where were you?'* Be still and listen for an answer.

PRAY:

Lord Jesus,
I thought you'd abandoned me,
but all the time you were there.
Help me not to doubt you in the dark times,
but to know that you're walking with me. Amen.

13 *In my place*

He couldn't believe it. He couldn't quite believe it. For months he'd been on the run, wanted for murder. Finally they'd caught him and he'd been condemned to die. Yet here he stood, a free man, at the back of the crowd, watching the preacher from Galilee being crucified in his place. He heard the nails being driven home. Heard Jesus say, 'Father, forgive them'. Saw the cross being heaved into place. Then it all got too much. He turned on his heel and went away. But as he did, it all flashed back . . .

READ:

[Pilate said to the crowd] 'I will have Jesus flogged, and then release him'. But they shouted back,'Away with him! Give us Barabbas!' (Barabbas had been thrown into prison for rioting in the city, and for murder.) Again, Pilate appealed to them, wanting to release Jesus. Again they shouted back, 'Crucify him! Crucify him!' . . . And Pilate decided to give them what they wanted. He released [the murderer] and handed Jesus over to them. (Luke 23:16–21, 24–25)

'In my place', thought Barabbas as he stood at the back of the crowd watching Jesus die. And he was right. But gradually the penny dropped in the minds of Jesus' followers. He'd died in their place too. Paul writes that 'God demonstrates his own love for us in this: While we were still sinners, Christ died for us' (Romans 5:8).

Jesus had done nothing evil in his whole life (even when he got angry). Yet on the cross he willingly took on himself all the evil we've done. Our sins smothered and suffocated him: such is the fatal power of sin. And Jesus bore the consequences of our sin. It killed him. But in taking our sin to the grave, Jesus killed its power. He rose from the dead to prove it. So whoever comes to Jesus, asking for forgiveness, will find that he is spared sin's fatal outcome. He has crossed over from death to life. He is forgiven. He begins a new life, that will never end.

 **Look at the picture of Barabbas. Write *your* name in the space provided.**

PRAY:

Did you really have to die, Jesus?
Was there really no other way?
Then I'll look at my sin with new eyes

14 *Tearing the curtain*

It's Friday November 10th 1989. I've just watched the historic pictures coming back from Berlin. After nearly thirty years of forcibly dividing the city, East Germany has opened up the Berlin wall. People are pouring through into the west. Champagne is flowing. There are sparklers everywhere. Crowds are dancing and singing on the wall itself. And everywhere there is a tremendous feeling of joy and hope. The iron curtain is melting!

History, of course, will judge whether these events are for the best or not. But two thousand years of history have treasured the demolition of a very different sort of curtain. In the temple, in Jerusalem, was a small room. It was called the Holy of Holies. Only one person, the High Priest, was allowed to go in. And even he could only go in once a year. Everyone else was kept out. This was the place where God was . . . nobody was good enough to enter God's presence . . . and so the Holy of Holies was curtained off from the rest of the temple.

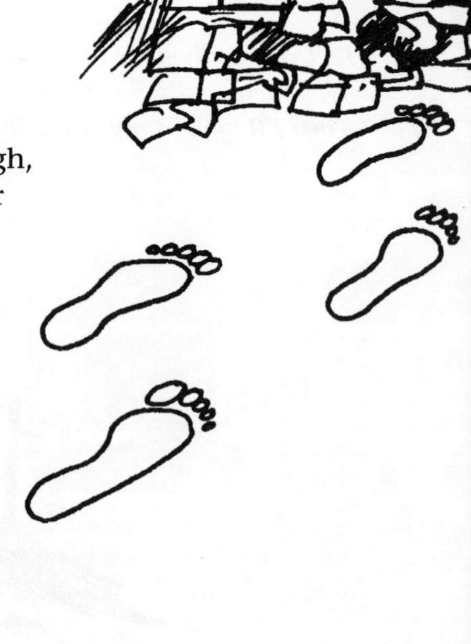

When Jesus died on the cross, though, God used this curtain to give us a clear visual aid to understand his death . . .

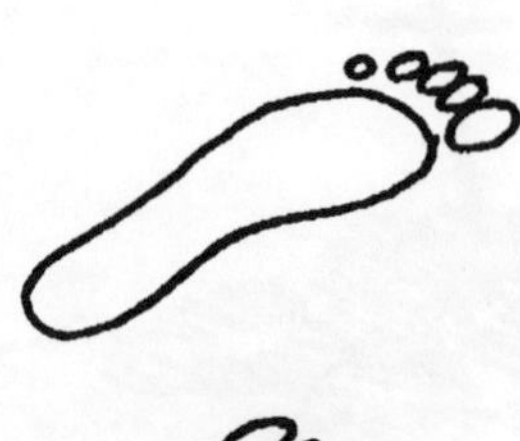

READ:

When Jesus had cried out again in a loud voice, he gave up his spirit. At that moment the curtain of the temple was torn in two from top to bottom. (Matthew 27:50–51)

Jesus opened up the way to God. He died to take away our sins. There is no longer any curtain between us and God. The barrier has gone! And everywhere there is a tremendous feeling of joy and hope.

GOD

☐ **The dividing wall has been broken down. We are free to go to God. Shade in the footprint that best shows where you are in your journey towards him.**

PRAY:

Father,
thank you that the dividing wall has gone
and that there is nothing to keep me from you.
Help me not to draw back,
but to come to you with confidence. Amen.

15 *He's not here!*

Peter sat in a corner, his head in his hands, his eyes screwed up tight. His mind went back to the upper room. Jesus had said they would all desert him. As usual, Peter had opened his big mouth. 'Never, Lord! I'll never leave you! I'm ready to die with you!' 'Before the cock crows, Peter, you will deny me three times.'

The echoes in his mind got too much. Peter jumped up and nervously paced up and down. But he couldn't shut them out. Now he was in that courtyard, warming himself by the fire. 'You're one of his followers!' 'No I'm not.' 'Yes you are. You're a Northerner aren't you?' 'I've never met the bloke!' 'I'm sure I saw you with him.' 'Look! I don't know what you're talking about. I don't *know* the man!' Then the cock had crowed. Jesus had turned and looked at Peter, his eyes full of love and sorrow. Peter's eyes filled with tears. He struck his forehead with his fist. 'How *could* I have done it!'

The day that Jesus died was crushing for his followers. Not only had a few of them watched their friend in agony on the cross, but they knew that at the end they had all let him down. Yet something happened. Something so special that that band of defeated men and women was changed. Within weeks they were risking death themselves by joyfully proclaiming that Jesus was alive again. That the grave had been unable to hold him. That he had snapped the chains of death. Peter must have been beside himself with joy. This is what he later wrote . . .

READ:

Let us give thanks to the God and Father of our Lord Jesus Christ! Because of his great mercy he gave us new life by raising Jesus Christ from

death. This fills us with a living hope, and so we look forward to possessing the rich blessings that God keeps for his people.
(1 Peter 1:3–4)

His mother and his friends had buried Jesus. They knew he was dead. But three days later they met him. They knew he was alive again. The resurrection of Jesus shouts to all the world that death cannot defeat the life of God. Because God brought life out of death. Thank God for that.

The real question of course is, 'Did it happen?' You must be the judge of that. There's plenty of good evidence. Look at this list and rank each piece of evidence in order of the impact it makes on you.

JESUS MUST HAVE RISEN FROM THE DEAD BECAUSE . . .

- ☐ *If his enemies had taken the body, they could have displayed it to scotch the rumour of Jesus' resurrection.*
- ☐ *If the disciples had taken the body they would have known their message was a lie.*
- ☐ *Something happened to change the disciples from frightened, hiding liars into a group prepared to risk death to proclaim that Jesus was alive.*
- ☐ *Over 500 people said they saw him alive.*
- ☐ *The four gospels all have eye-witness accounts of meeting the risen Christ.*
- ☐ *People the world over and down the ages say they've met him.*

PRAY:

Lord Jesus,
thank you that death could not hold you.
Thank you for the hope of Easter.
When things get hard and
I'm tempted to give in,
please help me to find
fresh hope in you. Amen.

16 *Please come home*

He lived for that sound—the postman's foot, the rattle of the letterbox, the rustle of the morning's letters on the mat. He lived for it. When it came, he ran to the door and snatched up the post. Full of hope, he shuffled through the pile . . . but nothing. No word. No news. Nothing.

Sitting back at the table, he ran his thumb under the envelope. But his mind wasn't on the job. He was somewhere else: 'Where is my son? Is he alright? Will he ever write? It's been two years now. Will I ever see him again?' That's how it feels waiting for news of someone who's run away from home.

We watched the prodigal son leave home in chapter five. And Jesus doesn't tell us much about the father who waited at home. But can you imagine a single day when his thoughts would not turn to his son? Who knows how many times he looked up to peer down the road, searching for a glimpse of him. And one day he got one. He couldn't be sure at first, because he'd changed so much . . . but was it? Surely not! It was! It was his son! Sadly making his way home . . .

READ:

'And when his father saw him, he was filled with hurting love for him, and running out he threw his arms around him and kissed him . . . "Put a ring on his finger, and sandals on his feet! Let's celebrate! With a feast! This son of mine was dead, but now he is alive again! He was lost, but now he has been found!" '
(Luke 15:20, 22–24)

God is longing for you to come home. And when you do, he is overjoyed. All the while you're away from him he scours the road, waiting for you, because he loves your company. And when he sees you coming he runs off down the road to meet you, and throws his arms around you.

God's message is still the same. To those who are far away from him today he says: 'I love and miss you. Please come home.'

Your son has left home. He's been gone for three years. You've heard nothing. In the box below write him a message telling him how you feel, and inviting him home.

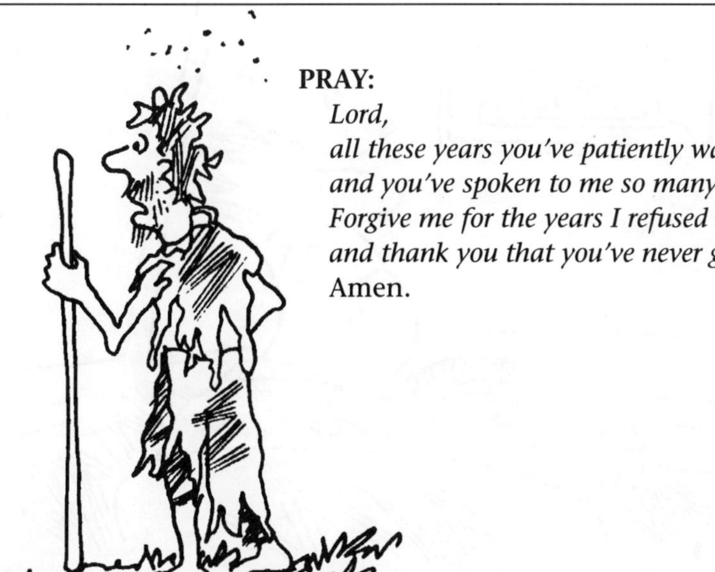

PRAY:

Lord,
all these years you've patiently waited,
and you've spoken to me so many times.
Forgive me for the years I refused to listen,
and thank you that you've never given up.
Amen.

17 Clean again

Graham was going to be late. He looked at his watch. He already *was* late. The lights were at red. A quick glance either way. A quick stab at the accelerator and he was through. Then, only then, he looked in his mirror (actually, the flashing light caught his eye). He was being followed. By the police.

For three long years his licence had carried the scars of his foolishness: another endorsement, yet more points—taking him to the brink of being banned. But at last the time had come. He'd sent his licence off to Swansea and now a long brown envelope lay on the doormat. He ripped it open. His licence was CLEAN AGAIN! And he punched the air in triumph and relief.

Moments of knowing that God has forgiven me have been among the very best of my life. To kneel before him knowing that I've failed. To say 'sorry', from the heart . . . and then to feel release from guilt as God is true to his promise to forgive . . . All this is

normal Christian experience. God gives us a completely new start when we first come to him. And then he goes on forgiving, whenever we fail and are truly sorry. So it makes no sense to try and hide our guilty secrets from him. He knows us better than we know ourselves. He wants to set us free.

READ:

If we say we have no sin, we deceive ourselves and the truth is not in us. If we confess our sins, God is faithful and just, and will forgive us our sins and wash us clean from every kind of wrong. (1 John 1:8–9)

☐ **In the box below, write a list of things you'd like forgiveness for.**

Now say 'sorry' to God.

Then take a different colour pen and write over your list the words we read just now: *'If we confess our sins, God is faithful and just, and will forgive us our sins and wash us clean from every kind of wrong'.*

PRAY:

There's no point hiding from you, is there?
After all, you know me better than I know myself.
Help me, then, to confess my sin with honesty,
and to receive the new start you long
to give me. Amen.

DVLC
CLEAN LICENCE

18 *Energy for life*

Have you ever run out of petrol? Embarrassing isn't it! You're driving along and suddenly there's nothing there. All you can do is phut-phut into the side of the road. It's only happened to me once. I was working at a hostel for young offenders, and had just taken one of the lads to court. Driving back to Bristol . . . nothing. And passers-by were treated to a rare spectacle: 'Punk Pushes Trainee Vicar Down Road In Mini'.

God calls us to live in a different way. But we don't have to rely on our own resources. If we do, we very soon end up empty by the roadside. God knows that when it comes to following Jesus we can't do it without his help. So he gives it to us . . .

READ:

[Jesus said to them] 'Wait for the gift my Father promised . . . [for] in a few days you will be baptised with the Holy Spirit . . .[and] you will receive power when the Holy Spirit comes on you.' (Acts 1:4–5, 8)

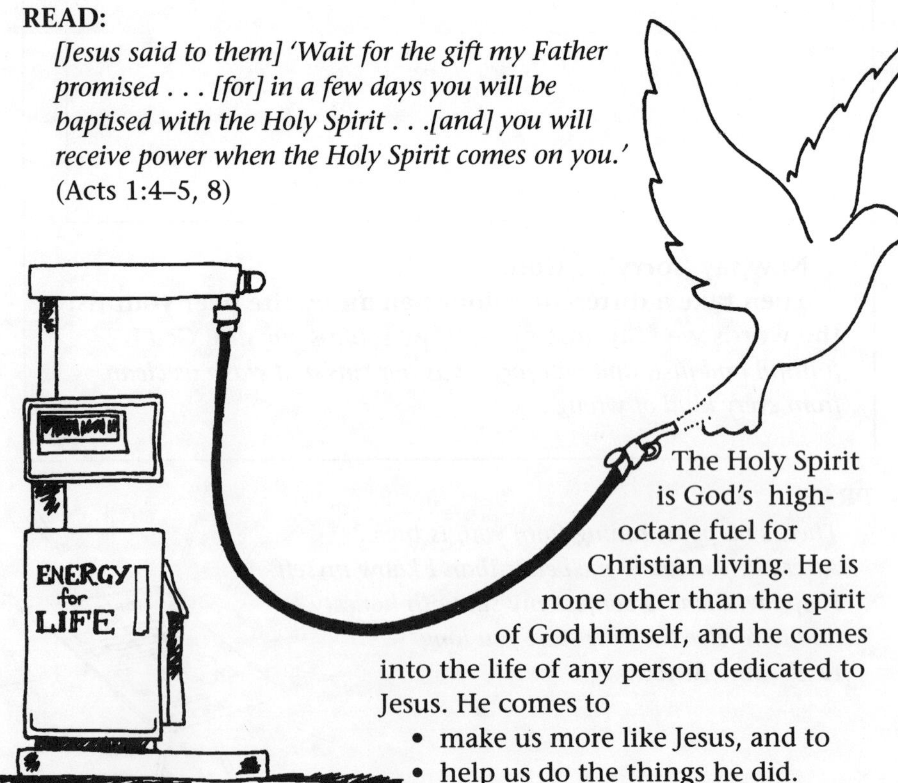

The Holy Spirit is God's high-octane fuel for Christian living. He is none other than the spirit of God himself, and he comes into the life of any person dedicated to Jesus. He comes to

- make us more like Jesus, and to
- help us do the things he did.

Do not attempt to follow Jesus in your own strength. Ask God to to flood you with his power. And then go on asking. 'Go on being filled with the Spirit', and he will change you, day by day, to be like Jesus. 'The one who calls you is faithful, and he will do it' (1 Thessalonians 5:24).

Hidden in this square of letters are the nine qualities that Paul calls 'the fruit of the Spirit'. These are things that the spirit of Jesus grows in the life of a Christian. List them in the space provided. (Galatians 5:22–23 in the Good News Bible wording may help.)

S	I	B	P	E	A	F	N	S	H	P	K
S	S	T	A	F	V	R	Y	S	K	A	G
E	G	E	H	U	M	T	O	E	I	T	E
N	R	S	N	R	I	Y	P	L	N	I	S
D	T	A	P	L	L	K	E	F	R	E	T
N	O	J	I	G	U	D	R	C	O	N	E
I	J	M	A	D	Q	F	J	O	Y	C	C
K	U	E	L	E	M	U	H	N	L	E	A
H	P	E	R	T	L	B	U	T	O	G	E
S	S	E	N	D	O	O	G	R	I	W	P
H	W	R	E	N	V	Y	D	O	F	A	K
G	O	K	N	L	E	T	A	L	O	J	F

Now look at the list and ask yourself, 'Which of these qualities do I need most?' Then ask God to give you that fruit, by his Spirit.

PRAY:

Holy Spirit, I feel so empty sometimes:
weak, powerless, and unable to change.
And so I open myself to you.
Flood me with yourself,
and make me more like Jesus. Amen.

19 *Two on a bike*

There was once a vicar, who was also a keen 'biker'. And this vicar, it seems, was always just on the right side of the law. Once, this revving reverend was enjoying a drink in the Pig and Whistle, when in walked the local bobby. 'One of these days we'll get you,' said the policeman to the vicar, 'and when we do, we'll throw the book at you'. 'Oh no you won't', said the vicar to the policeman, 'because the good Lord rides with me'. The constable's eyes lit up. 'Got you already!' he said. 'Two on a bike and no helmet!'

Two on a bike . . . and no helmet. That's a perfect picture of life following Jesus. Together you will ride into the future: a future as yet undiscovered. There will be risk. (Jesus never said that following him would be easy. You can get a lot of stick for trying to be a Christian.) But the master will be with you. That's certainly what the early disciples found . . .

READ:

As Jesus was walking by the Sea of Galilee, he saw Simon, and Andrew [Simon's brother] casting a net into the sea—they were fishermen. Jesus said to them, 'Come with me, and I will make you fishers of men'. And immediately they left their nets and followed him. (Mark 1:16–18)

Do you think those early disciples found it easy? To leave their nets meant leaving everything behind. From now on, all that they would have would be Jesus as their master. But he gave their life a purpose, and that small band of people turned the world upside down.

Today, Jesus is calling you. He wants you to follow him: you don't know where. He wants to change the world through you: you don't know how. It's a life of risk and challenge. How will you respond?

You'd expect a disciple of Jesus to be . . .

Honest and truthful	
Working for justice in the world	
The first to end a family row	
Slow to criticize others	
Generous with their time and money	

Shade in the bar to the extent that you think you match up to these descriptions.

PRAY:

Me? I disciple of Jesus?
Well, you've called stranger people in the past.
So . . . yes. I rise to the challenge.
I'll follow you, Lord, wherever you lead me.
Please change the world through me. Amen.

20 *Right where I belong*

'My Mum and Dad often used to tell me how special I was. When I was five or six I can remember them saying that I was special because they came and chose me. As I got older, though, the penny dropped: my Mum and Dad weren't my real Mum and Dad. I was adopted.

'Over the years it began to bother me more. There'd be family rows and my brother and sister would say, "You're not really Mum and Dad's anyway". I came to really hate my real Mum and Dad . . . to feel angry that they'd just abandoned me.

'Then when I was seventeen I became a Christian. And two or three years later I heard a sermon about being accepted into God's family. It was then it clicked. I'd been adopted twice over, and on even better terms than before. I'd been adopted by my heavenly father.

'The preacher's voice melted into the background then, and I had a vivid mental picture of a courtroom. Jesus looked at me and said, "Come here: I want to talk to you". There, on the desk in front of him was a set of adoption papers, with my name on. And I watched as Jesus himself signed them.

'I've never been able to forget that moment. It was so special. I know I'm part of God's family.'

Fay's story is special because she was 'adopted twice over'. But we can all share part of her experience: when we become Christians we too are adopted into God's family . . .

READ:

Those who are led by the Spirit of God are sons of God. For you did not receive a spirit that makes you a slave to fear, but you received the spirit of adoption. And by him we cry, 'Father, my Father!'
(Romans 8:14–15)

Look at the diagram below. Write your name in the centre. Then in each of the six outer places write the name of someone you know in your church.

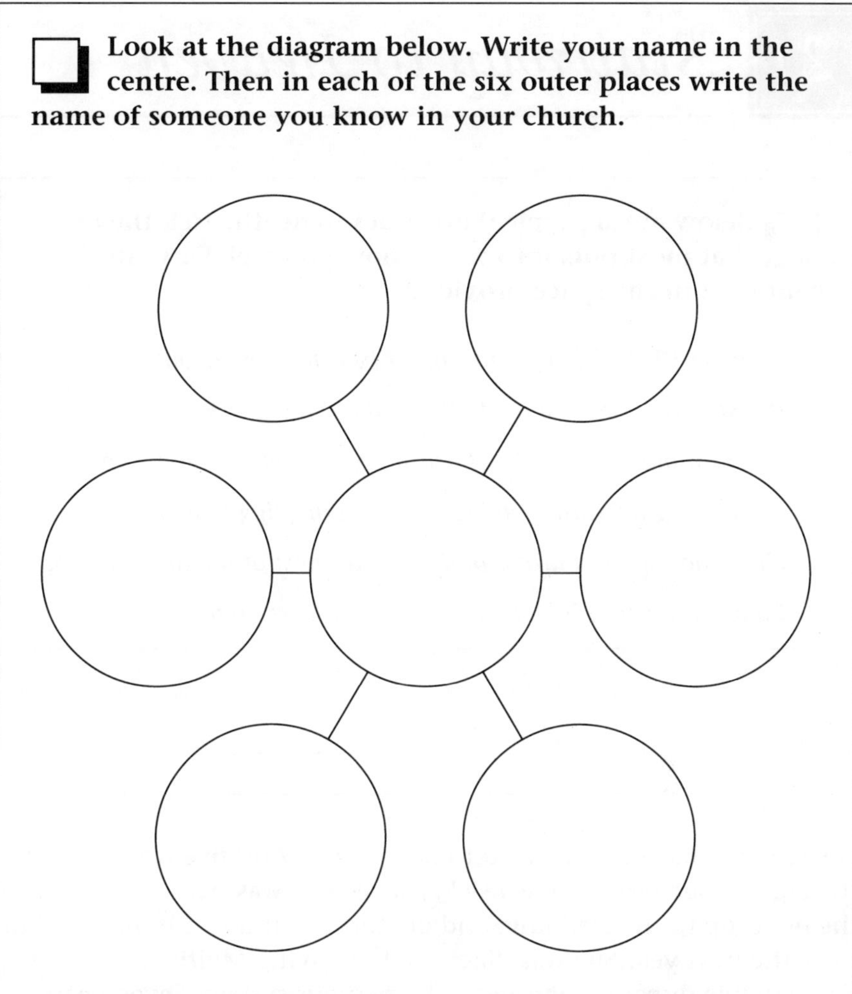

Now pray for these six members of your new family.

PRAY:

Father,
thank you that when we come to you
you adopt us as your children.
Thank you that you are our perfect father,
and that you receive us into the church, our second family. Amen.

21 *Stairway to Heaven*

Below are six typical attitudes to death. Tick the one that most puts into words how you feel. Or write your own in the space provided.

- ☐ *I am petrified of dying and cannot bear to think about it.*
- ☐ *It just never occurs to me to think about my death.*
- ☐ *I don't mind the thought of death because when you die you die.*
- ☐ *I'm looking forward to dying because I'm going to a better place.*
- ☐ *Now and then I'm afraid of dying, but most of the time I'm OK.*
- ☐ *I don't want to think about it, thank you very much!*

Stewart and Sue were engaged to be married. And five weeks before the big day Sue began to feel sick. Indeed she was sick—every day in the build-up to the wedding, and doctors put it down to nerves. But early the next year Sue was diagnosed as having Multiple Sclerosis, an incurable disease that attacks the nervous system. Seven years later she is very poorly. Yet recently she was able to dictate these words:

'The resurrection of Jesus means far more to me now, and gives me great comfort to know I shall be well and with him when I die. When I told my GP this he was dumbstruck and didn't know what to say! Now, I am much worse, but much more aware of what Jesus did for me. Although there are sad times, I know that Christ is with me and that he went through hard times too. So although I shall really miss Stewart and Naomi, I shall be glad to be in heaven and be completely healed. The resurrection means this promise for me.'

Why is it that Christians like Sue are able to face death with such courage and dignity and hope? Sue herself put her finger on it just now. It is because Jesus rose from the dead, defeating death once and for all. So the Christian knows that death is not the end. God's promise, to those who receive it, is that death is the beginning of a new kind of life. A life that will never end. A life spent with God in heaven.

READ:

Jesus said . . .'I am the resurrection and the life. Anyone who believes in me will live, even though he dies. And whoever lives and believes in me will never die.' (John 11:25–26)

PRAY:

Lord Jesus,
you know that sometimes I'm very afraid of death.
Give me, I pray, an Easter faith.
Faith that you have conquered death.
And faith that you did it for me. Amen.

22 *Turn round!*

I must be a glutton for punishment. I actually parted with ten pounds of good money to watch England play cricket. The day dawned grey and drizzly, we got held up on the motorway and finally got to Manchester with precious little time to spare. We left the M63 and at the roundabout took the most likely looking exit. Then, just too late, we saw a sign: 'Old Trafford Cricket Ground'. It was pointing in the opposite direction.

When you realize you're going the wrong way, the only thing to do is to turn round—especially when time is running out. But that's exactly what Jesus saw from his carpenter's shop: crowds of people going the wrong way—ignoring God and shutting him out of their lives. That's why this was his first message . . .

READ:

'The time is right! The Kingdom of God is close to you. Repent! And believe the good news.' (Mark 1:15)

'Repent' is a word that's had a bad press. It makes us think of sack-cloth and ashes and misery. Nothing could be further from the truth. To repent means to change your mind and turn round. It involves turning from the emptiness of my life to discover the much better life that God has for me. Jesus' followers preached the

same message: 'Repent, then, and turn to God, so that your sins may be wiped out, and that times of refreshing may come from the Lord' (Acts 3:19).

We don't repent in order to squeeze all the joy out of life. It's the exact opposite. We turn to God to discover a joy we can't find anywhere else. After all, 'life' was his idea. Turn to him, and *really* learn how to live.

In this book we've been following the story of the Prodigal Son. We've seen that there is a bit of the Prodigal Son in all of us. Think about his travels . . . and yours. Whereabouts on the journey are you? Tick the box that says it best . . .

- ☐ *Running away from your father God.*
- ☐ *Living in the distant country having a good time.*
- ☐ *Beginning to sense your need of him.*
- ☐ *Just getting up to come home.*
- ☐ *On the way back.*
- ☐ *In the arms of your father.*

PRAY:

Lord,
it makes such sense to turn round.
My way leads only to emptiness and death.
But you are the way to life and peace.
I turn to you. Amen.

23 Decision time

In the boxes provided, make a note of the three most important decisions you have taken in your life . . .

Playing rugby for Halifax thirds against Wibsey, I span the ball out to Steve. And Steve was caught in at least four minds. Should he go to the right? Should he go to the left? Should he make a break? Or should he kick? He spent so long thinking about it that it was clear he was about to buried by the Wibsey back-row forwards. Now Steve is a man with a sense of humour, and just before the crunch he had time for a broad grin and a mock groan of panic . . . and *then* he was buried by the Wibsey back-row forwards.

Decisions, decisions, life is full of decisions. 'Mark, will you take Joanne to be your wife?' . . . 'I think it's time for a move' . . . 'Let's start a family!' If you've followed this book from the beginning, you've been brought face to face with the most important decision of your life: 'Shall I follow Jesus? Shall I become a Christian?

Shall I get up and go home to the God who is waiting for me? Shall I turn round, and go his way instead of mine? Or shall I remain as I am, and ignore his call?'

READ:

[Jesus said] 'Go in through the narrow door, because the wide door with its broad road leads to destruction and there are many people going through it. But the door to life is narrow, and way leading to it is narrow too, and only a few find it.' (Matthew 7:13–14)

Jesus is calling you to make a decision. A decision for or against him. Do you want to decide for Christ? To choose life? Make this prayer your own . . .

PRAY:

Father God,
thank you for opening the door
and calling me home.

Father God,
I want to come home.

Forgive the wrong in my past
and help me to follow Jesus.
Fill me with your Holy Spirit
and adopt me into your family.

I give my life to you.
Help me to live for you.
And at my death,
take me to be with you in heaven.
Amen.

24 *Reading the Bible*

When people become Christians, they often feel that God is very close. In the months and years that follow, we need to keep in touch with him. There are four ways in which we can do that: by reading the Bible, by praying, by staying part of his family, the church, and by enjoying the service of Holy Communion.

Sometimes, people feel a bit put off the Bible to begin with. So let's take a deep breath, and ask three basic questions . . .

1. *What is the Bible?* The Bible is no ordinary book, it's

- A library, of sixty-six books, written over many years, by men and women who had met with God.
- A message, from God to you. It tells the story of what God is like, and of what he does for the world he loves.
- A blueprint, outlining the kind of life God wants you to lead.

2. *Why was it written?* To help us believe. Here's how the Bible explains it . . .

READ:

Jesus did many other miraculous signs . . . which are not recorded in this book. But these are written that you may believe *that Jesus is the Christ, the Son of God, and that by believing you may have life. . .* (John 20:30–31)

3. *How do I read it?* The Bible is in two main parts . . .

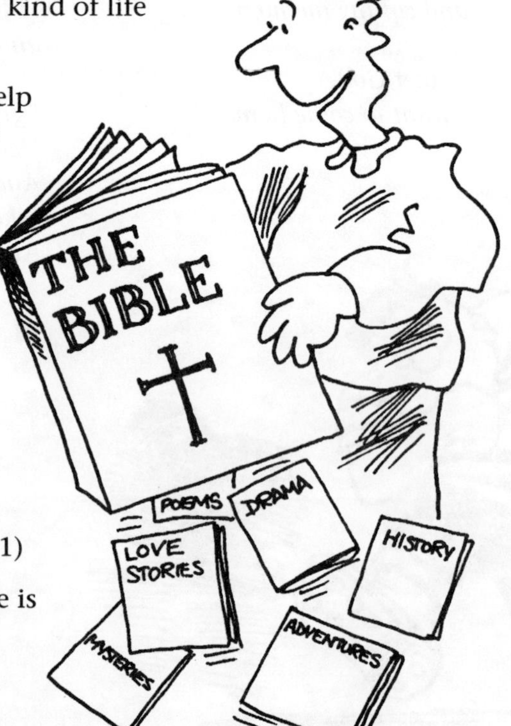

- The Old Testament, telling the story of God's people before the birth of Jesus.
- The New Testament, telling the story of the life of Jesus, and of God's people after his resurrection.

DON'T START AT THE BEGINNING! The Old Testament is more difficult to understand, and best left till later. The best place to start is with the life of Jesus. And the best book to start with is the gospel of Mark. Here's a sample passage (Mark 1:40–45) . . .

'A man with leprosy came to Jesus and begged him on his knees, "If you are willing, you can make me clean." Filled with compassion, Jesus reached out his hand and touched the man. "I am willing," he said. "Be clean!" Immediately the leprosy left him and he was cured.

'Jesus sent him away at once with a strong warning: "See that you don't tell this to anyone. But go, show yourself to the priest and offer the sacrifices that Moses commanded for your cleansing . . ." Instead, he went out and began to talk freely, spreading the news. As a result, Jesus could no longer enter a town openly but stayed outside in lonely places.'

Now fill in the boxes . . .

	Something I don't understand
	How God is asking me to change
	Something Jesus shows me about God

P.S. Make sure you get an answer to what's not understood.

PRAY:

Lord God,
thank you for the Bible.
Help me to understand the things I find difficult.
Change me, through all that I read.
And show me clearly who you are. Amen.

25 *Living Word*

In our wedding service, a passage from the Bible was read out. Since that day, our marriage has known its ups and downs, like any other marriage. And it's especially in the 'downs', when we've had a row and are fuming silently in separate rooms, that this passage hits home:

READ:

Therefore, as God's chosen people, holy and dearly loved, clothe yourselves with compassion, kindness, humility, gentleness and patience. Bear with each other and forgive whatever grievances you may have against one another. Forgive as the Lord forgave you. And over all these virtues put on love, which binds them all together in perfect unity. (Colossians 3:12–14)

It's very hard to read those words and stay the same. And that's the point. Those words were written to peel off my layers of anger and resentment, to rekindle my love, push me through into the next room and say, 'I'm sorry. Please forgive me.'

The Bible is alive. It is no ordinary book. It reaches out and grabs me by the scruff of the neck. Through it, God loves me, tells me off and trips me up. The Bible promises me things, opens my eyes to the suffering of the world and kicks me into action. It makes me a better person, a better husband, a better father. It rummages through my pockets, tells me to 'phone my Mum, and calls me to work for justice.

Why does it do all those things? Because God does all those things! The Bible's alive because God's alive. Thank God for the Bible.

☐ Because there is simply so much Bible, it's been broken down into smaller chunks. Each book is divided into chapters (the large numbers in bold print) and verses (the smaller numbers, often slightly raised). These three things (book, chapter, verse) make up what is called a Bible reference. So the thirty-fourth verse of the eighth chapter of Mark's gospel becomes *Mark 8:34.* (The books are listed in order at the front of each Bible.)

Colossians 3:13

Acts 2:38

Isaiah 41:10

John 5:24

Philippians 4:6

Tick the verse that speaks to you most clearly. Write it out then learn it . . .
And bring it back to mind when things get hard today.

PRAY:

So . . . the Bible's alive!
I've never really seen it like that before.
Give me, I pray, such a love for your book,
that I may hear you speaking clearly through it. Amen.

26 *Teach us to pray*

kHe had been hired to paint the Lord's Prayer onto a wooden board in the church. He stood back to admire his handiwork, and then saw that he was running out of space. Indeed, he did run out of space. His first line read 'Our Father, who art in heaven, hallo'.

Prayer is simply talking with God. He made us to love him, and a love affair is nothing without conversation. At the heart of love is talking and listening: a growing relationship. Our life of prayer is a vital part of our relationship with God.

When shall I pray? Whenever suits you. Some like to pray first thing in the morning. Others last thing at night. It doesn't matter. Just make time to be quiet with God. Jesus did . . .

READ:

Very early in the morning, while it was still dark, Jesus got up, left the house and went off to a solitary place, where he prayed. (Mark 1:35)

What shall I say? Anything. Anything that comes to mind. Tell him about your hopes and fears, in your own honest words.

Here's a rough outline to help you get started:

- Take some time to be quiet.
- Picture something beautiful. Think of God's delight in making it.
- Now thank God, for the good things in life.
- Then say 'sorry' for the ways you've hurt him and other people.
- Then pray for others, for the needs of the world.
- Then pray for yourself: ask God to meet *your* needs.

And remember, God is your perfect father. He is 'always more ready to hear than we to pray'. Prayer is not a chore. It's a conversation. A real, living conversation.

Things to thank God for:

Things to say 'sorry' for:

Things to ask for others:

Things to ask for myself:

PRAY:

Lord,
I still feel a fool when I hear myself praying.
But help me to relax
and to speak with you face to face. Amen.

Does God answer prayer?

Two-year-old Andrew stood in the kitchen and eyed the rows of jars with longing. 'Raisins please, Daddy', he said, and soon he was happily munching his way through a handful of raisins and Daddy was the best person there ever was. Then his eyes wandered to the next jar. 'Peanuts please, Daddy.' Daddy looked down at him. 'No, not peanuts, Andrew; they'd make you choke.' Andrew stomped off. 'Humph! I knew my Daddy didn't love me really.'

A lot of people treat prayer like that. They are thrilled and delighted when God gives them what they ask for . . . and then go off in a huff when he doesn't, and doubt that he really loves them, or worse still, that he's there at all. But God sees things from his point of view. He wants what is best for us. So he doesn't give us everything we ask for. He gives us what he knows we need most . . .

READ:

This is the assurance we have in approaching God: that if we ask for anything according to his will, he hears us. (1 John 5:14)

God knows our needs best. He knows them better than we do ourselves. So yes, he hears our prayers. And yes, he answers them. But the answer won't always be 'yes'. Sometimes the answer will be 'no', and sometimes the answer might even be 'wait'.

A little girl told her friends she was praying for a bicycle for Christmas. She went out to play on Christmas morning and they asked, 'Well then, did God answer your prayers?' 'Oh yes', came the firm reply . . . 'he said, "no".'

On the grid below write in the left hand column the things your are praying about. Then go on praying for these things. When a month has passed, come back to your list. Put a tick in the middle column if you think your prayer has been answered. Then make a note in the right hand column of how you think it's been answered . . .

Things I'm praying for:		*How God answered:*

PRAY:

I'm listening to you, Lord.
Or at least, I'm trying to.
Please give me the confidence to ask,
the patience to wait, and
the wisdom to hear you clearly. Amen.

28 The Body of Jesus

Life is not meant to be lived alone. When we become Christians, God adopts us into his family. Paul says that that family is like a human body . . .

READ:

Now the body is made up not of one part but of many . . . If the whole body were an eye, where would the sense of hearing be? If the whole body were an ear, where would the sense of smell be? But in fact God has arranged the parts of the body, every one of them, just as he wanted them to be . . . You are the body of Christ, and each one of you is a part of it. (1 Corinthians 12:14, 17–18, 27)

Just imagine it. You walk into a room and there's just this great ear lying on the floor. It can hear a pin drop, certainly, but it can't move! It just lies there, wriggling pathetically. You're out for a walk when suddenly this massive eye rolls past you down the hill. You turn in amazement. It can *see* that wall coming up, but it's powerless to stop
and—SPLAT! Oh dear.

The human body is made up of hundreds of different organs . . . but they all make up one body. It's the same with the church. We're all different. We're all unique. We all have different gifts, different strengths, different weaknesses. We've all got different jobs to do in the family of the church. Together we 'are' Jesus to the world.

So. Two ground-rules of being in the church.

- Firstly: don't try and be like anybody else . God loves you just as you are.
- And secondly: play your full part. No one else in the church has exactly your strengths. The church would be weaker without you.

Your local body of Christ needs *you.* One of the ways in which we grow as Christians is to offer our time and talents to God in practical service. When we do, it's not only us who benefit: the whole body of the church is helped.

Look at the list below and ask yourself if you could meet any of the suggestions. (Then contact whoever's in charge!)

Visiting the elderly or disabled.
Joining the church drama group.
Helping with the Mums and Toddler group
Reading the lesson in church
Delivering the parish magazine
Cleaning the church building
Playing a musical instrument in the worship
Acting as a sidesperson in your church
Teaching the children on a Sunday
Preparing parents for their child's christening.
(The list goes on: from bereavement care to typing . . .)

P.S. Some of these things are *best* done by new Christians.

PRAY:

Thank you for the church, Lord.
Thank you that we can all play a part.
Help me not to imitate anyone but you
and to play my full part in the Body of Christ. Amen.

29 . . . Broken for you

Jesus knew that the time had come. In a matter of hours he would be arrested, given a mockery of a trial, and killed. So he gathered his friends together for one final meal . . .

READ:

The Lord Jesus, on the night he was betrayed, took bread, and when he had given thanks, he broke it and said, 'This is my body, which is [given] for you; do this in remembrance of me.' In the same way, after supper he took the cup, saying, 'This cup is the new covenant in my blood; do this, whenever you drink it, in remembrance of me.' For whenever you eat this bread and drink this cup, you proclaim the Lord's death until he comes. (1 Corinthians 11:23–26)

Picture the scene. They sit there in the candlelight. Suddenly Jesus takes a loaf, tells them it is his body . . . and rips it apart. He pours wine into a cup and tells them it is his blood. They look from one to another, and quietly eat and drink. How *could* they understand what Jesus meant? But the penny began to drop the following day, as his body was being broken apart on the cross, and his lifeblood began to slow and stop. And as his followers struggled to understand the cross they began to realize that this last supper was saying: 'God loves you so much he would die for you'.

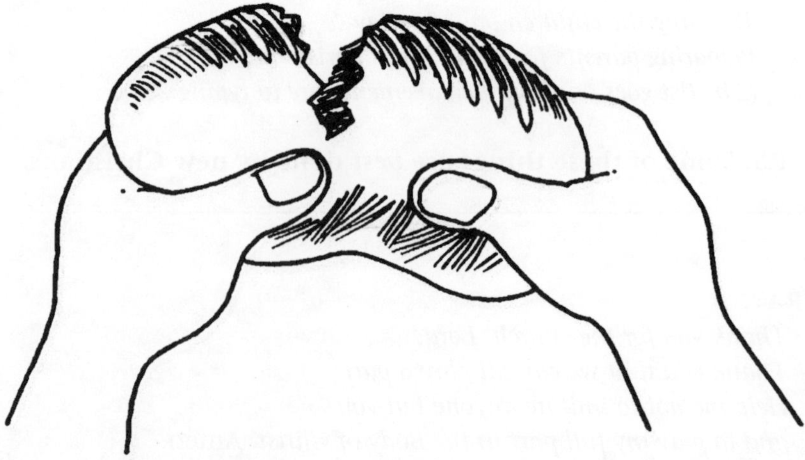

Christians the world over still 'do this in remembrance of me'. They call it Holy Communion, or the Eucharist, or the Lord's Supper, but it doesn't matter what you call it. The important thing is that by bread broken and wine poured out we 'proclaim the Lord's death until he comes'. We remember that he died. We remember why: his death brings us forgiveness. As we receive the bread and wine together we share the love of God in a way that goes beyond words. This Communion with God is Holy. It's central to Christianity. It should be central to your Christian life.

❑ There are many things to discover in the Communion service. It takes a lifetime to discover and fully understand them. But the more we prepare for Communion, the more we're able to give (and receive) in the service.

Here's a 'Communion Preparation Kit'. Try and make time to work through the checklist before you go to Communion.

Take time to look at the week just gone.
Think*: in what ways have I hurt those around me?*
Prepare to confess them in the service.

Have a moment's quiet.
Think*: is there anybody I need to forgive?*
If so, forgive them, asking God for the strength to do so.

Take time to look ahead to the week to come.
Think*: what particularly hard moments or decisions do I face?*
Ask God to equip you for them in the service.

PRAY:

Thank you, Lord, for these pictures of your love:
the bread broken and the wine poured out.
Help me to prepare myself properly for Communion,
and to meet with you in the service. Amen.

30 The weapons of love

Margarida is a Brazilian widow. She has five children. Every morning she gets up at three o'clock and walks six miles to work. There, she spends four hours heaving rocks to build a dam. Her monthly pay is £8. 'When I leave home, I have a bit of coffee with manioc flour, that's all. Hunger pains begin by about ten o'clock but you have to put up with them. The ones who can't just collapse. I've seen lots of women collapse onto the rocks. We earn next to nothing, but my work is the only thing between us and death.'

Margarida is not alone. Millions like her lie at the bottom of the pile, trapped by the massive injustice of the world. You're probably near the top of the pile. Most people reading this book will be well fed, clothed, watered and housed. Meanwhile . . .

- Ten children a minute die of diarrhoea.
- Six out of seven people do not have clean running water.
- 35,000 people a day die because they haven't enough food.
- And every fortnight, the world spends £12 billion on arms.

Our God is a God of justice. He burns with anger at suffering caused by human greed and folly. He wants you to share his anger, and work with him for a fairer world . . .

READ:

'Is not this the kind of fasting I have chosen: to loose the chains of injustice and untie the cords of the yoke, to set the oppressed free and break every yoke? . . . If you spend yourselves on behalf of the hungry and satisfy the needs of the oppressed, then your light will rise in the darkness, and your night will become like the noonday.'
(Isaiah 58:6, 10)

You have joined God's army. He wants you to fight for what is right. With the weapons of love.

☐ **Look at this 'involvement' scale. Put a tick where you think you are now. And another where you'd like to be in six months' time.**

Unaware of world issues. ☐

Beginning to find out more. ☐

Actively wanting to find out more. ☐

Beginning to realize that I can do something. ☐

Knowing I can do something but wondering what. ☐

Writing to my MP. ☐

Supporting an aid agency with my money. ☐

Supporting an aid agency with my time. ☐

. . . .

PRAY:

Lord, there's so much to do isn't there?
So much to say. So much that's wrong with the world.
But help me to do my bit, however small,
to make the world a fairer place. Amen.

31 *You did it for me*

You don't have to look abroad, of course, to find people in need. There's the elderly widow, trapped and alone in her high-rise flat. There are the parents of the mentally handicapped teenager, desperate for a rest and a break; the single parent with two demanding toddlers on her hands all the time. There's the crash victim, in his wheelchair, who'd love to see Manchester United play again; the fifty-year-old spinster dying of cancer in the local hospice. We are surrounded by people in need. The follower of Jesus cannot ignore them . . .

READ:

'[They] will answer him, "Lord, when did we see you hungry and feed you, or thirsty and give you a drink? When did we see you a stranger and invite you in, or needing clothes and clothe you? When did we see you sick, or in prison, and visit you?" The King will reply: "I tell you the truth. Whatever you did for one of the least of these brothers of mine, you did for me".' (Matthew 25:37–40)

Our good works don't get us to heaven. But God does expect that our love for him will blossom out into service of others. So take a good look round your community. What particular needs are there? Listen to God's prompting as you read the Bible, and pray, and meet with other Christians. What is he calling you to do? It may be visiting an old people's home or a mental

hospital. It may be inviting a lonely person to come and share a meal with your family. It may be to stand as a local councillor, to let the voice of God be heard in public life.

Whatever it is, do it with joy—you're serving your master, Jesus. He trod the path of the servant. We're privileged to follow in his footsteps.

☐ **Look at the table below. Do you know any of the kinds of people described? Write down their name. Then, in the right-hand column make a note of a practical way you could help.**

A lonely, elderly person . . . . *Someone who cares full-time for a handicapped relative* . . . . *A disabled person* . . . . *A single parent with demanding children* . . . . *Someone with an incurable disease*	

☐ **So. We've arrived. But in a sense the journey's only just begun. Look back through your booklet. Which unit meant most to you? *Thank God for that!***

PRAY:

Father God,
thank you for this book,
and for all you've shown me through it.
Here I am, Lord. Go on teaching me. Go on guiding me.
Go on using me to change the world.
And help me to share the good news of your love. Amen.

32 What next?

'Be sure to keep in touch!'—we say it to new friends we've met on holiday, and to old colleagues we've met again after a gap and found to be well worth knowing. 'Keep in touch' means 'Let's not leave it too long before we're enjoying each other's company again!'

THANK GOD FOR THAT has encouraged a real, personal contact with God our Father. It has done this as we've read 31 Bible readings and prayed 31 prayers . . . Let's keep the pattern going. Each day, surely, we can afford the time for a Bible reading and some prayer! In this way we meet and listen to God our Father in company with all who love and trust Jesus. The result is a a guided life, a purposeful succession of days in which we express our gratitude and are strengthened to live responsibly.

☐ **Make sure you follow a Bible-reading scheme. Ask your local church leaders, or contact the Bible Reading Fellowship (address opposite) for details of its regular Notes. (Some Notes have passages printed out, others are for use with a Bible; all include suggestions to help with prayer.) Keep in touch!**